Acclaim for

FA▌▌▌

"*Fado* is a triumph. ▌▌▌
long after the fi▌▌ ▌▌▌▌ are sung."
—NIKO MUMFORD, *Showbill Canada*

"★★★★★ *Fado* hits high notes ... Cinema-style at its best ...
expressing the pains which come from the heart and soul."
—*Otaku no Culture*

"In a world filled with diaspora and people attempting to
reconnect with what was left behind – people, place, culture –
Fado resonates and pulls at heartstrings in inexpressible ways."
—JANIS LA COUVEE

"Splendid, multilayered, *Fado* is a new pleasure. It speaks of
history, politics, music, identity, mother–daughter relations
with extreme mastery. Well done, well done, well done!"
—MARC FOURNIER, Radio-Canada Première

Praise for Elaine Ávila's Plays

"Tremendously gifted, reliable, and innovative ...
a great joy. Elaine Ávila is a wonderful writer."
—SUZAN-LORI PARKS, Master Writer Chair,
Public Theater, New York

"You simply must see this show. Absolutely ... touching,
exciting, and surprisingly funny. Cancel whatever evening
plans you may have to go see this show while you can.
I guarantee people will be talking about it for years to come."
—*Monday Magazine*

ALSO BY ELAINE ÁVILA

Plays

Jane Austen, Action Figure and Other Plays

Lieutenant Nun and Other Plays

Lighting the Way: An Anthology of Short Plays about the Climate Crisis (edited by Chantal Bilodeau)

Monologues for Latino/a Actors: A Resource Guide to Contemporary Latino/a Playwrights for Actors and Teachers (edited by Micha Espinosa)

Scenes for Latinx Actors: Voices of the New American Theatre (edited by Cynthia DeCure and Micha Espinosa)

24 Gun Control Plays (edited by Caridad Svich and Zac Kline)

Where Is the Hope? An Anthology of Short Climate Change Theatre Plays (edited by Chantal Bilodeau)

Essays in Anthologies

Antologia literária Satúrnia: Autores luso-canadianos (edited by Manuel Carvalho)

Casting a Movement: The Welcome Table Initiative (edited by Claire Syler and Daniel Banks)

Innovations in Five Acts: Strategies for Theatre and Performance (edited by Caridad Svich)

Stages of Resistance: Theatre and Politics in the Capitalocene (edited by Caridad Svich with Olivia George)

FADO

The Saddest Music in the World

by Elaine Ávila

Foreword by Oona Patrick

Afterword by Mercedes Bátiz-Benét

Appendix by Lila Ellen Gray

Talonbooks

Talonbooks
9259 Shaughnessy Street, Vancouver, British Columbia, Canada V6P 6R4
talonbooks.com

Talonbooks is located on xʷməθkʷəy̓əm, Sḵwx̱wú7mesh, and səlilwətaʔɬ Lands.

First printing: 2021

Typeset in Minion
Printed and bound in Canada on 100% post-consumer recycled paper

Cover design by Typesmith, interior design by andrea bennett
Cover photography by Derek Ford

Talonbooks acknowledges the financial support of the Canada Council for the Arts, the Government of Canada through the Canada Book Fund, and the Province of British Columbia through the British Columbia Arts Council and the Book Publishing Tax Credit.

LIBRARY AND ARCHIVES CANADA CATALOGUING IN PUBLICATION

Title: Fado : the saddest music in the world / by Elaine Ávila ; preface by the author ; foreword by Oona Patrick ; afterword by Mercedes Bátiz-Benét ; appendix by Lila Ellen Gray.
Names: Ávila, Elaine, 1965– author. | Patrick, Oona, writer of foreword. | Bátiz-Benét, Mercedes, writer of afterword. | Gray, Lila Ellen, 1966– contributor.
Description: A play. | Play in English; includes some text in Portuguese.
Identifiers: Canadiana 20200334654 | ISBN 9781772012897 (SOFTCOVER)
Subjects: LCSH: Fados—Drama.
Classification: LCC PS8551.V535 F33 2021 | DDC C812/.6—dc23

Para Arlina Garcia da Terra Ávila,
Minha Queridinha Avózinha

Music was my refuge. I could crawl
into the space between the notes
and curl my back to loneliness.

—Maya Angelou, *Singin' and Swingin' and
Gettin' Merry like Christmas* (1976)

If you penetrate the seduction of
the city, then it becomes possible
to confront your own history.

—Toni Morrison, *Toni Morrison:
Conversations* (2008)

Fado was invented by the Portuguese.
They did it for a reason. Why?
Because of their nature.

—Amália Rodrigues in *The Art of Amália,*
film by Bruno de Almeida (2000)

Contents

Preface: *Já não voltam* xi
Foreword by Oona Patrick: Lisbon Journey xv

Production History xix
List of Characters xxi
Setting and Time xxii

Fado: The Saddest Music in the World

Prologue: *Fado* 3
Lisboa 7
Maneira de ser 11
O Miradouro da Graça 17
O ferro a vapor 24
Os sapatos 28
A tasca 35
As ruas 44
A fundação 48
O museu 54
A andorinha 58
Inúteis 62
Estranha forma de vida 65
Fado 66
Tristão 70
Tudo isto existe 71

Afterword by Mercedes Bátiz-Benét 73
Appendix: Four Amálias: Voicing Drag,
by Lila Ellen Gray 77

Endnotes 81
Glossary 83
Further Reading, Viewing, and Listening 86
Acknowledgments 89

Rosida (Lucia Frangione) receives a visitation from the Ghost of Amália (Sara Marreiros) while ironing, making sure her daughter's clothes are up to Lisbon's formal standards. Many of Amália Rodrigues's devoted fans report feeling comforted by Amália's presence as they sing along with her iconic recordings, especially during the loneliness of household chores. (Photo: Derek Ford)

Já não voltam

Elaine Ávila

I slip into my theatre seat, incognito. It's easy to be invisible: many, sadly, still can't comprehend that a woman could be the playwright, affording me the chance to anonymously hear how an audience is responding to my play. I find myself sitting next to a young couple, who tell me they are recent immigrants from Iran.

Listening to audiences, for a playwright, is a delicious treat, and a duty, because I learn from the listening: how to improve my work for the next draft, for the next play. Plays are like children. Some need much, others give back immeasurably. Some travel the world without you; some take you along on their adventures. This play needed much, gave much, and took me along. But it also robbed me of my usual anonymity. As I sit next to the couple, the man speaks.

MAN

(*confiding*) I'm so excited. (*gesturing to his companion*) She knows how much I love theatre, so she surprised me with the tickets. Isn't that romantic? She also knows how much I love fado. I LOVE it! Isn't she great?

ME

(*smiling at them*) Yes.

The female companion smiles, knowingly.

They remind me of my grandparents, how they might have been, when they were young.

MAN

(*looking at his program, where there is a small picture of me*)
Wait? Aren't you the playwright?!

ME

(*nodding, shyly*) Yes.

MAN

I can't believe the night got even better! We are so lucky!
What an honour!

ME

(*blown away by their charm, unable to say something self-deprecatory, which is my habit*) Uh. Thank you. I hope you
enjoy it.

After the lights dim, they listen, they laugh. But as the play progresses, he begins weeping, openly, more and more, and his companion passes him tissue after tissue, until he reaches out for another tissue to mop up his eyes again, and she shakes her head. None left. Then I listen to the entire audience, a sold-out crowd, nestled around me in the dark. They are all weeping. The actors, who'd done a beautiful job, come out for their bows, and the audience applauds. The lights come back up.

MAN

(*joking, referring to his tears*) Happy?

I smile sheepishly, sharing that I hadn't expected so many people to cry. Then he begins pouring his heart out to me, about his experience immigrating, which lines in the play he related to, and what forbids immigrants and refugees from telling their stories openly. They both invite me for dinner.

This couple became emblematic of the audiences for this play – quick on the uptake, observant, generous, excited for a night on the town, curious about what was lost to their families through migration, and, at times, picking up that I was inspired by my collaborations with Inuit and First Nations artists to unearth stories and songs from my own culture.

This play gave me so many experiences like this one. If it was one of my offspring, it was certainly a big-hearted one, making friends, sharing deep conversations. The play sold out nearly every performance for a month, and then, invitations to tour began pouring in from across Canada and the United States. Then the COVID-19 pandemic happened. Theatres shut. I became even more grateful for having met this couple by chance, being in a theatre where audiences could laugh and cry together. Talonbooks offered to publish the play, and I welcomed the chance to continue the conversation.

Fado is the first Portuguese play by a lusodescendant to play a major stage in the U.S. or Canada. Any "first" like this owes much to the people who supported it and those who came before, those who fought and wrote about the prejudice against us, which is why there is, happily, a robust acknowledgment page at the end of this volume. Thank you. The wonderful collaborations that made this play could fill a book of their own – exploring late-night fado clubs with skilled Playwrights Theatre Centre dramaturge Kathleen Flaherty, who suggested I learn to sing fado, which I did as an artist-in-residence at Quest University in the snowy mountains above Squamish, British Columbia ... searching for the very saddest fado song in the world during a dramaturgical process with director Mercedes Bátiz-Benét of Puente Theatre (author of this book's afterword) and her actor husband Judd Palmer, huddled over laptops, in their cozy home in Victoria ... a candlelight dinner in an intimate Greenwich Village restaurant with fado scholar Lila Ellen Gray (see this book's appendix) who told me about her research in drag clubs ... Donna Spencer, Susan Shank, and the staff at the Firehall Arts Centre in Vancouver, who gave this play a home replete with outreach to the Portuguese community, which donated / put up posters / came out to see the play from insurance shops, coffee bars, food-import centres, community bakeries and groceries ... winning the Portuguese playwriting contest at the Disquiet International Literary Program in Lisbon, co-founded by Oona Patrick (author of the foreword in this book), which helped me tap into the new power of finding other lusodiasporic writers, sharing passionate conversations in Lisbon's winding streets.

I dedicate this play to my grandmother, Arlina Garcia da Terra Ávila, for her bravery in leaving her small village of Ribeiras, Lajes do Pico, in the Azores, to make a new life with my grandfather, João Henrique Ávila, never knowing that those beautiful days in her village, as she wrote, "já não voltam" (would never return). Thank you to Nlaka'pamux actor, artist, activist, and writer Stephen Lytton, who told me that he thought I could make those days return. Thank you to my grandfather, who played me my first fado record when I couldn't understand why I had never learned a single Portuguese song. Then he confided that he had sung fado in the Portuguese Hall in San Diego, California, opening for the Queen of Fado, Amália Rodrigues. I thank Amália Rodrigues, who would have turned one hundred and one this year, prompting celebrations across Portugal and online, for showing the world that peasant girls can become writers and artists. And thank you, dear reader, for being willing to go on this journey back to Portugal, to see if we can rediscover what we lost.

This play is an homage to fado music. As you read, I invite you to pull up YouTube or Spotify or nestle in close to your turntable, whatever you use to listen to music, and explore the songs referenced in the play. Listen to the great Amália Rodrigues, Mariza, Argentina Santos, Ana Moura, Carlos do Carmo, Camané, Maria da Fé, Cristina Branco, Carminho, Gisela João, Mísia, António Zambujo, Carlos Saura's 2007 documentary *Fados*, Sara Marreiros (who starred in our production) ... Crank it up. Light some candles, drink a beverage you would find in a fado club – red wine, *vinho verde* (or effervescent green wine), mineral water, passion-fruit soda, or *limonada* (lemon juice, water, and sugar to taste). *Bem-vindo*. Welcome.

Lisbon Journey

Oona Patrick

I'm sitting on a beach in Provincetown, Massachusetts, where I've been marooned by pandemic in my childhood home, rereading Elaine Ávila's *Fado*. It's a five-minute walk from here to the site of an old wharf where American theatre was supposedly born in 1916. Legend has it that on the opening night of Eugene O'Neill's debut play, *Bound East for Cardiff*, even the fog joined in, rolling from across the harbour as if on cue. Nevertheless, reading *Fado* here today, all I can see and hear is the city of Lisbon.

Elaine's play is one of the best explorations of a Portuguese descendant's return journey to that city that I've ever read. I've witnessed dozens of writers of our shared background take this journey every summer since 2011 (every summer, that is, until now). I've taken to calling *Fado* a lusodescendant epic, as it turns the struggles and structure of those return trips into a greater quest for identity and meaning.

I first met Elaine in 2014 when she won the Disquiet International Literary Program's first Short Play Contest. She came to Lisbon with our summer literary program first as a prizewinner and later as faculty. There, up to a hundred mostly North American writers spent two intense weeks in workshops and engaging with the local literary scene. About a quarter were of lusophone-country descent and were at various stages of searching for family roots or cultural ties in Portugal.

One memorable evening after Elaine first arrived, local actors performed her prize-winning short *Café A Brasileira* in a landmark theatre next door to our headquarters at the Centro Nacional de Cultura. I didn't know her well yet, but I still remember the pride I felt watching her sketch parts of the Portuguese Canadian experience, centring long under-represented characters, something I'd never seen on stage before. For this reason, I felt like crying even at the funny moments, something I think many audiences of *Fado* understand. As a fellow writer, I was also in awe of her winsome, bittersweet dialogue and wordplay, and how her scenes homed in on the awkward, lonely, and funny incidents in travel. The neighbourhood also seemed to be giving her gifts, like O'Neill's fog: yellow Number 28 trams rattled by every few minutes, and we were a block or so from the real Café A Brasileira, close enough to think we could hear the street musicians playing their guitars.

With her recent play *Fado*, Elaine has captured the obsession and mixed feelings of the new community of lusodescendant writers that emerged in our program. Like Rosida in the play, they or their families had often longed to see Lisbon, but didn't, so to speak, have shoes for the trip. Though the majority had ties elsewhere – in rural areas, the islands, or former colonies – they came to a consensus that their journeys somehow had to go through Lisbon.

In the mornings, in the program's workshop focused on the Luso-American experience, I listened to enthralled, slightly wild-eyed writers recount the adventures of the day before. They told of hearing first-hand about life under the secret police from a taxi driver, and then huddling around a political prisoner's tiny cell in the Museum of Aljube – Resistance and Freedom; reading the plaque on a long-awaited memorial to an Inquisition massacre, and then visiting an active synagogue; learning that women writers had had a hand in bringing down the dictatorship, and then meeting one of them; and, perhaps most memorably, coming upon Lisbon's Gay Pride march in a city square, and then sobbing by the Tagus River because they'd never felt this welcome before in Portugal.

The experience of the city tells of the fight to take up space; many of the program's resulting poems, stories, essays, and plays are about this. A number of writers, notably playwrights, are claiming more space for LGBTQ+ themes, especially, in lusodescendant writing and simultaneously in Portugal. Elaine's character Rui captures this ongoing work toward breaking silence, and how it connects people across cultures. While he is not on a return journey like Luisa and Rosida are, Rui has nevertheless been finding himself, a bond the cousins share in Lisbon.

With all there is to learn in the city, some of the most important moments are those of unlearning falsehoods. This is exemplified in the play by the discovery that the "Uma casa portuguesa" fado had been used as propaganda by the Salazar regime. Previous generations hadn't had access to the full story, or sometimes refused to pass it on. "I only know what they taught us in school. The glory of Portugal. We discovered the world," Rosida says near the end of scene 6. In Lisbon, writers soon find themselves asking big questions they couldn't ask at home, such as what role might their ancestors have had in slavery, in the Inquisition, in centuries of oppression, either as victims or tormentors. One's identity comes a bit unstitched.

Fado nights are a pivot in these trips; going uphill into the storied Alfama neighbourhood to hear fado led to some of the most intense reactions the next morning. It was a rapturous, semi-private passage nearly everyone went through, as if there were a door in the hillside of Alfama, and that door was fado. It led to what most were trying to access: the past. Sometimes the euphoria of the beginning of the trip turned to melancholy, a realization of how much one had missed, how much one had to learn, and how difficult it would be to truly reconnect. The word *saudade* went without saying in this group; it was simply understood.

At the end of *Fado*, the play's themes dovetail into the problem that many confronted when they descended from Alfama and came down from these heightened experiences. What next? How does one make art out of this particular pain? After the joy of discovery, many found they'd complicated things for themselves, added another layer of misfit. Like Luisa, some longed to change everything, to recentre their lives in Portugal, a move that felt more and more impossible once they returned home. "I don't belong anywhere," says Luisa. *Fado* ends with Luisa finally able to express this new way of being in song.

After nine years of going to Lisbon, I have come full circle back to the beach where I grew up, holding a gorgeous play that speaks directly to me about my experience. I'm still yards from that famous wellspring for Anglo-American theatre, where family legend tells me my great-uncle, a labourer on the town wharves, served as an extra in the background of O'Neill's debut that night on the pier – just another silent Portuguese fisherman. But so much feels different now, because of writers like Elaine. Maybe this journey had to go through Lisbon, maybe not. I know only that the city, inaccessible once more, continues to give me gifts, and Elaine is one of them.

Production History

Fado: The Saddest Music in the World was first produced by Puente Theatre at the White Eagle Polish Hall in Victoria, British Columbia, from August 23 to September 2, 2018, with the following cast and crew:

AMÁLIA	Sara Marreiros
ALEXANDRE, on guitar	Dan Wise
LUISA	Finn Letourneau
ROSIDA	Cyllene Richmond
RUI and AMALIANA	Pedro M. Siqueira
TRISTÃO	Chris Perrins
ANTÓNIO	Judd Palmer

Director	Mercedes Bátiz-Benét
Stage Management	Emma Dickerson
Costume and Set Design	Patricia Reilly
Lighting Design	Emma Dickerson
Sound Design	Aidan Dunsmuir
Costuming	Hannah Carr
Additional Sewing	Pauline Stynes
Wig Styling	Cristina Woods
Makeup Mentoring	Elizabeth Newman

The play was remounted by Puente Theatre and the Firehall Arts Centre at the Metro Studio in Victoria from November 14 to 16, 2019, and at the Firehall Arts Centre in Vancouver, British Columbia, from November 21 to December 14, 2019, with the following cast and crew:

AMÁLIA	Sara Marreiros
ALEXANDRE, on guitar	Dan Wise
LUISA	Natércia Napoleão
ROSIDA	Lucia Frangione
RUI and AMALIANA	Pedro M. Siqueira
TRISTÃO	Chris Perrins
ANTÓNIO	Judd Palmer

Artistic Producer	Donna Spencer
Director	Mercedes Bátiz-Benét
Stage Management	Emma Dickerson
Costume and Set Design	Patricia Reilly
Lighting Design	Emma Dickerson
Sound Design	Aidan Dunsmuir
Costuming	Hannah Carr
Additional Sewing	Pauline Stynes
Wig Styling	Cristina Woods
Makeup Mentoring	Elizabeth Newman
Scenic Carpentry	Yong Shian Sam and George Scott
Additional Set Painting	Carole Klemm

Characters

Three women, three men

LUISA, a recent university graduate and emerging singer
ANTÓNIO, Luisa's fado teacher in Lisbon and one of Portugal's finest guitarists
ROSIDA, Luisa's mother
TRISTÃO, a Portuguese writer
RUI, Luisa's long-lost cousin, later as AMALIANA, *fadista* drag queen
AMÁLIA, a ghost, the Queen of Fado
BAND MEMBERS

Setting

A bare-bones space such as a theatre, warehouse, or music club. Like at a music concert where each song evokes a world, each setting is created simply, fluidly, by adding a set piece, a prop, a sound cue, a projection, a lighting cue, or a costume.

Surrey, British Columbia, Canada: a run-down Canadian apartment.

Lisbon, Portugal: winding streets, Amália's house, a rented room, a *miradouro*, a museum, a drag club.

Time

October 1999 to August 2000.

FADO

The Saddest Music in the World

TOP: The Ghost of Amália (Sara Marreiros) holds the spotlight once more. Amália Rodrigues was born into poverty but nonetheless became the diva of all divas, singing in nearly every nation on earth. Every *fadista* (fado singer) pays a tribute to her whenever they sing a concert. (Photo: Derek Ford)

BOTTOM: Fado clubs in Lisbon have a special intimacy, an inviting coziness, an untranslatable feeling known as *acolhedor*. The singers and *guitarra* players (here, Judd Palmer, Dan Wise, and Pedro M. Sigueira) listen closely to each other. In turn, the audience listens to the performers and is sometimes invited to sing along, making the entire club a musical instrument. (Photo: Derek Ford)

Prologue: Fado

The ghost of the Queen of Fado, AMÁLIA
*Rodrigues, known throughout the world, enters
in a glamorous, floor-length black dress, as she
favoured in the 1970s, accompanied by her
three musicians, strumming fado guitar chords.*
AMÁLIA *smiles at the audience, sweeps her
arms out as if to embrace them, and sings. Her
song is an explosion of sentimento (feeling).
She sings one of her songs, "Grito" (meaning
a cry, scream, or call), one of the saddest
songs on earth. It begins with the words
"Silêncio! / Do silêncio faço um grito ..."[1]*

AMÁLIA *finishes the song in a crescendo
of emotion, raises her arms in triumph.
Applause. She and her band disappear.*

ROSIDA *enters, weeping and cradling
Amália Rodriques's 1982 album* Fado.
She sinks to the floor. LUISA *enters.*

ROSIDA
It's all slipping away.

LUISA
*Mãe,** what is?

---

* Translations of italicized Portuguese words, expressions, and quotations used in *Fado* appear in the end glossary, p. 83. Numbered notes to the play appear on p. 81.

ROSIDA
Amália Rodrigues. She died. Portugal is mourning, *por três dias*. Three days.

LUISA
Oh.

> *LUISA sinks to the floor, then looks
> at the Amália Rodrigues album.*

LUISA
You haven't played this since Dad died.

> *ROSIDA nods. They embrace. LUISA
> wipes her mother's tears.*

LUISA
Remember? When I was small, how you'd dress me as Amália, tease up my hair, put those huge sunglasses –

ROSIDA
– on your little face –

LUISA
– and we'd all sing fado?

ROSIDA
Ah, *querida*, we loved that. You were so cute. That was before we had to sell the house.

LUISA
How we'd shop at Union Market and the Drive, buy salted cod, *chouriço*, *queijo*, sweet bread, *pastéis*?

ROSIDA
(*nodding*) To cure our *saudade*.

LUISA

(*looking at the album*) *Mãe*, why is this record signed
personally to you?

ROSIDA

I grew up with him.

LUISA

(*reading on the album*) António Silveira? Amália's guitar
player. You. Grew. Up. With. Him?!

ROSIDA nods.

LUISA

What? *Mãe*, that's amazing. Write to him. Ask if I can learn
to sing fado music with him!

ROSIDA

What? No, no, it's been too long.

LUISA

Please? We could go together. We've always talked about
going back. Now's the time. I'll pay for everything. Work
double shifts.

ROSIDA

No, querida.

LUISA

Mãe, please. In university, I'm so grateful I studied Bach and
jazz and world music, but I didn't sing a single fado. I know
about hanging out at the mall, but nothing about the streets
of my ancestors. I've never been to Portugal. It's a home I've
never known. Please, *mãe*, I want to find my fado, before it
all slips away.

ROSIDA stares at LUISA, tears in her eyes, indecisive. LUISA holds her, then leads her off. Sound cue: the streets of Lisbon's Alfama neighbourhood; voices speaking in Portuguese, echoing off stone walls; the screech of a tram; birdsong; a distant church bell.

Scene 1

Lisboa

ROSIDA and LUISA enter with suitcases. They take in the city. ROSIDA is overcome with feeling for all she has lost.

ROSIDA
  Oh querida.

LUISA
  Mom?

ROSIDA
  Thank you.

> *LUISA beams with pride. She moves the suitcases into their rented room.*

ROSIDA
  (*grabbing LUISA's hand*) We're home.

> *LUISA nods, then looks at her watch.*

LUISA
  We have to go.

> *ROSIDA nods. She opens her suitcase and starts searching through it.*

LUISA
  We don't want to keep him waiting.

7

ROSIDA
(*searching more and more frantically*) We want to look our
best. *Querida*, where is the iron?

LUISA *looks guilty but says nothing.*

ROSIDA
I'm sure, I... packed it. Where is it?

LUISA
I took it out.

ROSIDA
You what?

LUISA
I took it out.

ROSIDA
Ai, Santa Catarina. Luísa Margarida! Why? Why would you
do this?

LUISA
I wanted you to relax.

ROSIDA
Relax? With wrinkled clothes. *Querida, a roupa suja lava-se
em casa!*

LUISA
Ai, Mom. It's not dirty. Just not perfect. Don't worry.

ROSIDA
We can't go out like this.

LUISA
Like what?

ROSIDA gives her a look.

LUISA
Mãe, we've got to go.

ROSIDA
No.

LUISA
What?

ROSIDA
I'm not going. Not like this. We must show respect!

LUISA
Oh, *mãe*. You look beautiful.

> *ROSIDA shakes her head. LUISA begins
> looking through the suitcases.*

ROSIDA
What are you doing?

LUISA
Trying to find something that's not wrinkled. Oh, forget it!
You even iron underwear.

ROSIDA
What's wrong with that? It feels good. *Ai!* We'll look like
peasants.

LUISA
What's wrong with being a peasant?

ROSIDA
Luisa! I worked my whole life to make sure we are no longer
peasants!

LUISA
Mom, Mom, please. Calm down.

ROSIDA
Don't keep him waiting. You go.

LUISA
But *mãe* –

ROSIDA
Go.

> *ROSIDA straightens* LUISA's *clothes, then collapses on a chair. She waves for* LUISA *to go.* LUISA, *reluctantly, leaves.*

Scene 2

Maneira de ser

ANTÓNIO Silveira, one of Portugal's finest guitarists, plays with one of his BAND MEMBERS in a fado club. LUISA enters. She interrupts.

LUISA
(*to the BAND MEMBERS*) Mestre Silveira?

The BAND MEMBERS gesture toward ANTÓNIO.

ANTÓNIO
Sim?

LUISA
Luisa. Luisa Carvalho.

ANTÓNIO
Prazer. (*moved*) Rosida. Your mother. I see her. In you.

LUISA
Uh. Thank you?

ANTÓNIO
Where is she?

LUISA
She's... jet-lagged, resting, overwhelmed.

ANTÓNIO
Of course.

LUISA

It's such an honour to meet you, sir. Thank you for agreeing to teach me.

ANTÓNIO

So, you sing?

LUISA

Yes.

ANTÓNIO

Fado?

LUISA

Yes.

ANTÓNIO

Very good. *Fala português?*

LUISA

Yes. *Mais ou menos.* I –

ANTÓNIO

Understand it better than you speak it. I know how it is for you. Many emigrants come back to reconnect with their roots, to search for what they have lost. Okay, okay. But… *O fado não se aprende. O fado não se explica.* (*to his* BAND MEMBERS) *O fado é uma maneira de ser.*

LUISA

Fado is… a way of being?

ANTÓNIO *nods.*

ANTÓNIO

Uma maneira de ser. Okay. Let's hear you sing. Name a song.

12

LUISA
"Uma casa portuguesa." Key of A. (*or whichever key she sings it in*)

> LUISA *sings "Uma casa portuguesa,"*
> *starting with the words: "Numa casa*
> *portuguesa fica bem / Pão e vinho sobre a*
> *mesa ..."*[2] *The rest of the* BAND MEMBERS
> *play, but* ANTÓNIO *freezes, refuses to*
> *play.* LUISA's *confidence improves as she*
> *sings, but she stumbles over a lyric here and*
> *there. She's learning, she has potential.*

ANTÓNIO
Never sing that song again.

LUISA
Why not?

ANTÓNIO
It's fascist.

LUISA
Fascist?

ANTÓNIO
It's propaganda. It should never, never be sung.

LUISA
But it's my mother's favourite.

> ANTÓNIO *shakes his head.*

ANTÓNIO
Ai. Rosida.

LUISA
What do you mean, it's propaganda?

ANTÓNIO
Listen to the lyrics.

LUISA
(*translating*) *Uma casa portuguesa*... A Portuguese house.
Pão, bread... *vinho*, wine... blue tiles, rosemary, roses...
They're just Portuguese things.

ANTÓNIO
Singers must understand the lyrics. You don't do this
in Canada?

LUISA
Yes – I –

ANTÓNIO
Lyrics are poetry!

LUISA
Yeah, I'm still learning, *mestre* Silveira. That's why I'm here.

ANTÓNIO
Go on.

LUISA
Dois braços, two arms that are waiting to embrace you... Oh.
No. *Alegria da pobreza*... (*stopping abruptly and turning to
the audience*) "The joy of poverty."

ANTÓNIO
So, the poor should never renounce the joy of poverty?
What a thing to say. What a thing to sell us. I'm a musician,
I play for everyone. I play anything. But we had to play
that song over and over. And who do you think loved

it the most? The fascists. The rich. Watching them raise their glasses, course after course, praise us for being good musicians, for uplifting the Portuguese, with roses and rosemary. The joy of poverty!

LUISA *is deeply shaken.*

LUISA
You lived through the dictatorship. What was it like, in those days?

ANTÓNIO
Your mother never told you?

LUISA
No.

ANTÓNIO
It is good you never knew such things. It was good for your parents to move away.

LUISA
I don't know about that.

ANTÓNIO
I am sorry, I must ask you to come again. The show is starting soon. Tomorrow?

LUISA
Yes, thank you.

ANTÓNIO
Bring another song. We will see what we can do with you.

LUISA
I will. Thank you again, *mestre* Silveira.

15

ANTÓNIO
(*exiting, then pausing*) Will your mother come, tomorrow?

LUISA
I am sure she will.

ANTÓNIO
Tell her I will be very happy to see her again.

LUISA
I will.

Scene 3

O Miradouro da Graça[3]

TRISTÃO is sitting on a small bench,
overlooking the city, writing in a notebook.
LUISA enters, pensive after her lesson with
António. She catches site of TRISTÃO: she
stops, finds him sexy, pretends not to, paces
one way, then the other, then decides to sit.

TRISTÃO
  Excuse me –

LUISA
  How do you know I speak English?

TRISTÃO
  We have a lot of tourists.

LUISA
  Oh god, is it obvious?

TRISTÃO
  Portuguese women –

LUISA
  What?

TRISTÃO
  Tend to wear different shoes.

LUISA
  Oh. (*laughing*) *Você é de Lisboa?*

TRISTÃO
Sim. How do you know I'm Portuguese?

LUISA
Canadian men –

TRISTÃO
What?

LUISA
Don't usually wear ironed clothes.

TRISTÃO
(*laughing*) Which part of Canada are you from?

LUISA
I'm from Surrey, British Columbia. I mean, Vancouver.

TRISTÃO
Oh, wonderful. Trees. Bears. Mountains. Glaciers! I wish I could see that.

LUISA
Maybe you can, someday.

TRISTÃO
Do you design your streets, how do you say, in *redes*? Mesh? Straight lines?

LUISA
In grids. In Surrey, the streets mostly have numbers, not names.

TRISTÃO
So you never get lost.

LUISA
  We still get lost.

TRISTÃO
  It seems...

LUISA
  What?

TRISTÃO
  Forgive me.

LUISA
  What? Say it.

TRISTÃO
  Unpoetic. Numbers. Streets in grids.

LUISA
  It is. Unpoetic. Very. But here, it's beautiful. The tourist
  brochures say Lisbon is one of the oldest cities on earth.
  So many people have walked on these ancient stones, and
  yet it stays intimate. The city wraps around you with a
  cosiness, each turn in the street leading you to a story,
  unfolding between people. My dad died when I was young,
  but I can feel him here, in these streets, more than I ever
  have. And my mother, I can imagine what she longed for
  when she was young, and my ancestors before them, and
  before them... Here I feel like what I do might matter,
  might add a mark, leave an echo... of something wonderful.
  (*gesturing to show the beauty of the ancient streets
  surrounding them*) How could we give this up for malls and
  stores that look all the same?

TRISTÃO
  But there must be a certain freedom to remake yourself?
  As whoever you want to be.

LUISA
Yes, I ... yes.

TRISTÃO
There is poetry in that.

LUISA
Yes. I'm Luisa Carvalho.

TRISTÃO
Ah. One of us. Nice to meet you, Luisa. *Muito prazer.* I'm
Tristão Gularte.

> *TRISTÃO goes to kiss both of LUISA's cheeks
> in a traditional Portuguese greeting. She is
> alarmed by this and puts out her hand to
> shake his. He smiles and shakes her hand.*

LUISA
What do you do, Tristão?

TRISTÃO
I write. Poems.

LUISA
You're a poet?!

TRISTÃO
Yes. That's why my clothes are ironed. I just came from a
reading.

LUISA
I've never met a poet.

TRISTÃO
Many emigrants had to leave Portugal for work. They had to
leave poetry behind. *Uma vergonha.* A shame.

LUISA
  Why?

TRISTÃO
  Poetry – it binds us to each other, to the earth, to the
  troubadours, to the bravery it took for us to venture out on
  the seas, into the unknown. You know, we had the longest
  dictatorship of modern times, but we overthrew it peacefully,
  with poetry, set to music.

LUISA
  No, I don't know. That's why I'm here.

TRISTÃO
  "On each corner, a friend / On each face, equality." Isn't
  that beautiful? That's "Grândola, Vila Morena" by Zeca
  Afonso,[4] the song that was the signal to the military to start
  the revolution. "On each corner, a friend / On each face,
  equality." A woman, Celeste Caeiro, put carnations in the
  barrels of the guns that day, and her act amplified, everyone
  joined in, almost no shots were fired. We call it *Revolução
  dos Cravos*, the Carnation Revolution.

LUISA
  Wow.

TRISTÃO
  How long are you staying? What will you go see?

LUISA
  I'm not here to do the typical tourist stuff. I'm here to
  sing fado.

TRISTÃO
  Ah. You're a *fadista*!

LUISA
Yes. I'm here to study it.

TRISTÃO
(*confused*) Can you study it?

LUISA
I know, (*sighing*) I know, you feel it.

TRISTÃO
Forgive me, but in your part of the world, it seems people are afraid of this. Of feeling. And especially of being sad.

LUISA
Yes, I suppose we are.

TRISTÃO
Then you are brave. To allow such feeling. I was wrong about you. You are not just a tourist.

LUISA
Thank you. I hope I'm not.

TRISTÃO
You feel deeply.

LUISA
Thank you. Where can I find your poems?

TRISTÃO
If you like, I can invite you... to the launch of my new book. Some of my poems are about *fadistas*.

> *LUISA sizes him up again, then nods and takes the invitation.*

LUISA
Yes. I'd love to.

TRISTÃO
Wonderful. I look forward to it very much.

LUISA
Me too.

Scene 4

O ferro a vapor

ROSIDA, her hair in rollers, is ironing.
AMÁLIA is watching her, stylishly holding
a cigarette, as if she's about to smoke it.
ROSIDA is humming "Uma casa portuguesa."
AMÁLIA joins in. ROSIDA sighs, stops, then
holds up the shirt, notices a wrinkle, and
irons some more. AMÁLIA kisses ROSIDA
on the forehead. ROSIDA is comforted
by her presence but does not see her.

ROSIDA begins putting on her makeup and
pulling her hair out of rollers and styling it.

LUISA enters and is jolted when she hears
ROSIDA singing "Uma casa portuguesa." LUISA
studies her mother carefully. Noticing LUISA,
both AMÁLIA and ROSIDA quietly cease
singing. AMÁLIA wanders and watches them.

ROSIDA
How did it go?

LUISA
(*evasive*) Fine. How's it going with you?

ROSIDA
Wonderful. Everyone says "*Bom dia!*" like they did when
I was a girl. Ah, Luisa, it's so good to hear Portuguese
again, to speak it, it's all coming back. And I found an iron!
Um ferro a vapor. When I saw the gleam of coppery pots in
the window, I knew I'd found the place. So old-fashioned.

I said to the gentleman working there, "*Por favor. Eu quero um ferro a vapor, senhor.*" He was so polite. He wrapped it so carefully, tied the package with string. So fancy… *É um luxo. Querida*, you know when I was a girl, we could not afford to make a trip into Lisboa. We couldn't afford such luxuries.

LUISA
You couldn't afford an iron?!

ROSIDA
Of course not.

LUISA
I didn't know we were *that* poor.

ROSIDA
Why should we tell you all the terrible things?

LUISA
Oh, *mãe*. I want to know what it was like! What it was really like! I want to know where I come from.

ROSIDA
Yes… (*an awkward silence, then changing the subject*) What happened at your lesson? With António.

LUISA
He was nice.

ROSIDA
Oh?

LUISA
He didn't like the song.

ROSIDA
What did you sing?

LUISA
Your favourite, "Uma casa portuguesa."

ROSIDA
What's not to like?

LUISA
He said it's fascist propaganda.

ROSIDA
What? It's about a mother's love! Making a home.

LUISA
Mãe, it says the poor should never renounce the joy of
poverty. You should listen to what the lyrics say, analyze the
contradictions.

ROSIDA
Ai. Well, I may have only gone to grade four, but I knew how
to get you through university.

LUISA
Why does the song say it's good to be poor?

ROSIDA
We were humble. We were close. We had to be.

LUISA
At least in Canada we don't have to say poverty's great.

ROSIDA
What do you know about poverty? Nothing! I made sure
of that. I worked my whole life... trying to give you a
better one.

LUISA
I know, Mom. Your life *made* my life.

ROSIDA

And your life made my life, too, *querida*. Everything makes sense because of you. We've made it.

> *ROSIDA finishes ironing, then holds out a coat for LUISA to take.*

ROSIDA

Here's your coat. It's time to go meet your cousin.

LUISA

You ironed my coat? *Mãe*, it's not the style. He'll think I'm some kind of princess.

ROSIDA

I hope so!

> *ROSIDA is perfectly coiffed. She adjusts LUISA until she is perfect. They exit.*

Scene 5

Os sapatos

Café Nicola, on Praça de D. Pedro IV, better known as Rossio Square. RUI is wearing very neatly pressed clothes. ROSIDA and LUISA enter. The three look at each other uncomfortably.

ROSIDA
  Rui?

> *RUI stands, then nods.*

ROSIDA
  Oh. Rui. (*taking RUI's face in her hands*) I see Carolina. I see my sister. Your mother. God rest her soul. I see her. In your eyes.

> *RUI starts to get tears in his eyes.*
> *LUISA looks very uncomfortable and doesn't know where to look.*

RUI
  Obrigado, tia.

ROSIDA
  Tia! Yes. I am your *tia.* (*taking his hands*) Carolina used to write me about you.

RUI
  Please, sit, *tia.*

ROSIDA
All the time.

RUI
I didn't know. (*suddenly noticing* LUISA) You must be Luisa?

LUISA
Yes, and you must be Rui.

ROSIDA
Yes! You are cousins!

LUISA
We know.

RUI
It's lovely to meet you, Luisa. My mother, God rest her soul, said you two had some hard times, but look at you now. *Duas princesas do Canadá.*

ROSIDA
Ah, Rui. I'm so happy. Look at you. Such a nice young man.

RUI
Obrigado, tia.

ROSIDA
Your mother – one day, she stopped mentioning you in her letters. Why?

LUISA
Mom!

RUI
I don't know.

ROSIDA
God rest her soul.

RUI
(*changing the subject*) Do you like it here?

LUISA
It's beautiful. But Rui, is this where the locals go? Where do *you* hang out?

RUI *laughs: he isn't going to say.*

ROSIDA
Luisa, no.

LUISA
Mom, no one is speaking Portuguese. It's full of tourists.

ROSIDA
Luisa, don't be rude.

LUISA
I want to see something real. Insider Lisboa.

ROSIDA
This is real. *Muito obrigada*, Rui, I love it. I've always dreamed of coming here. Café Nicola. With the fancy people of Lisboa. (*reading the back of the menu*) Look, Luisa, it was one of the city's first cafés.

LUISA
You couldn't afford to come here?

ROSIDA
Luisa, you had to have shoes to come to the city. And we didn't have shoes.

LUISA
(*feeling the journey her mother went through*) Oh, Mom.

RUI
Yes. Well. (*toasting like a salute*) To happier times. Even if there are a lot of tourists. Oh, dear. The waiters seem to be occupied. I'll order for us. *Cafés? Pastéis de nata?*

LUISA
Are they gluten-free?

ROSIDA
Luisa!

RUI
(*standing up*) I'll ask.

    RUI exits.

ROSIDA
Don't ruin this for me!

LUISA
(*to* ROSIDA) He's hiding something, don't you think?

ROSIDA
Hiding? He's a wonderful young man!

LUISA
Well, you were right about the ironing, I'll give you that.

    RUI returns with small espressos and pastéis.

RUI
I'm sorry, *prima*, they're not gluten-free. Do you still want one?

ROSIDA
Yes, she does.

LUISA
Obrigada. Oh my, it's delicious.

ROSIDA
Everything tastes better in Lisboa.

RUI
Prima, you are here to sing fado, is that right?

LUISA
Yes. I am.

RUI
Wonderful.

LUISA
Really?

RUI
Yes, of course!

ROSIDA
(*getting something from out of her bag*) Look what I bought!

LUISA
A... plastic travel mug, with a glow-in-the-dark... face of...
Amália.

ROSIDA
Do you love it?

LUISA
Yes. I love it.

> LUISA *catches* RUI's *eye ... who*
> *can't help laughing.*

RUI
It's amazing!

ROSIDA
And practical. (*pause*) Are you making fun of me?

RUI
We're not.

LUISA
We're not.

ROSIDA
(*hurt*) I thought you'd like it.

LUISA
I do! I love it!

RUI
Tia, I have the exact same *caneca de viagem*. I love Amália.

> ROSIDA *beams.* RUI *winks at*
> LUISA. LUISA *beams.*

RUI
Tomorrow let me take you somewhere I hang out.

LUISA
Oh yes, please. Where?

RUI
The Fundação Amália Rodrigues, her Casa Museu.

ROSIDA
Amália's house?!

RUI
Yes. My friends have made it into a museum. It's very special.
You like?

LUISA
We love it.

> *ROSIDA crosses herself.*

ROSIDA
Amália's house!

RUI
Até amanhã.

> *They nod, rise, and give each other*
> *Portuguese kisses goodbye (on both*
> *sides of the face).* RUI *exits.*

Scene 6

A tasca

LUISA is at her lesson with ANTÓNIO,
who accompanies her on the guitar. She is
singing Amália Rodrigues's "Barco negro
(Mãe Preta)," from her 1955 self-titled
album, starting with the words: "Eu sei, meu
amor, / Que nem chegaste a partir ..." [5]

ANTÓNIO
(*stopping abruptly*) This isn't a recital. You are imitating
Amália too much.

LUISA
But she's the best.

ANTÓNIO sighs, then nods.

LUISA
You must miss her.

ANTÓNIO
The whole city feels empty without her. Luisa, true, you
need to start by going to the source, understanding those
who came before you. But there is only one Amália. If we
can hear your love of Amália in your sound, it is wonderful.
But it must be your sound.

LUISA
Okay.

*She resumes singing, starting from the
beginning.* ANTÓNIO *stops again.*

ANTÓNIO
No feeling.

LUISA
But I AM feeling!

ANTÓNIO
What? What do you feel?

LUISA
I don't know. I'm thinking –

ANTÓNIO
Thinking?

LUISA
I'm sorry, I'm nervous.

ANTÓNIO
This song is about heartbreak, not thinking!

> *They start to play again.* LUISA,
> *flustered, resumes her singing.*

ANTÓNIO
(*interrupting once more*) Don't you know what it means to
have your heart broken?

LUISA
Of course I do!

ANTÓNIO
You're too young. You don't know great love.

LUISA
I've known great love!

ANTÓNIO
You don't know what it means to lose someone.

LUISA
Yes, I do. I lost my dad. He never saw me grow up. Never saw me sing a solo. Never saw me get my university degree. Yes, you can say I know nothing about the songs of my people. I studied Bach and Beethoven. But I do know heartbreak.

ANTÓNIO
(*chastened*) Of course, of course you do. I'm sorry.

LUISA
It's okay.

ANTÓNIO
I heard it was an accident. At work.

LUISA
Did you know him?

ANTÓNIO
I only met him once, at the wedding.

> *Seeing LUISA's sadness, ANTÓNIO tries to come up with comforting words.*

ANTÓNIO
It was a… nice wedding. He seemed like a nice man.

LUISA
Yes, he was.

ANTÓNIO
Of course. Luisa, there are all kinds of heartbreak, for a love
that never came to be, or for the crimes of your country.
Do you know what I mean?

LUISA
Yes.

ANTÓNIO
This fado was banned. The original lyrics were censored.

LUISA
Why?

ANTÓNIO
The original song was from Brazil. It's about a Black mother,
forced to nurse the master's son while her own little boy
was being beaten. Salazar, the dictator, didn't want us
thinking about that. But when you sing, you must remember.
We listen between the lines, beneath the lines.

> ROSIDA *enters.* ANTÓNIO *sees*
> *her over* LUISA's *shoulder.*

ANTÓNIO
Rosida.

> LUISA *turns to see.*

ROSIDA
António.

LUISA
You came!

ANTÓNIO
It is good to see you.

ROSIDA
Yes. How have you been?

> ANTÓNIO *gestures around him, then shrugs.*

ROSIDA
It's nice.

ANTÓNIO
And you?

ROSIDA
Good.

> ROSIDA *steps next to* LUISA *and puts*
> *her hand on her shoulder, as if to say:*
> *"You can see in her how I am doing."*

ANTÓNIO
She is a lovely daughter. You did well to leave.

ROSIDA
Yes. (*with too much emotion to be believable*) I made the
right decision.

LUISA
(*confused*) How do you guys know each other again?

ROSIDA
(*to* LUISA) We grew up together. (*to* ANTÓNIO) Remember,
when they'd play those movies in the village hall?

ANTÓNIO
Of course I do.

LUISA
I thought there was no electricity.

ANTÓNIO
They'd power the movies by bicycle. Some poor fool in the
village would ride to keep the movies going. Heaven forbid
he should get tired.

ROSIDA
It was you!

ANTÓNIO
Yes.

ROSIDA
Remember that reel of Amália singing? I made you pedal
and pedal until I learned the words?

ANTÓNIO
Ha! Yes.

ROSIDA
António, and now you're an artist. You made something of
yourself.

ANTÓNIO
Obrigado.

ROSIDA
De nada. But, António, why do you say my favourite song is
fascist?

ANTÓNIO
Because it is.

ROSIDA
"Uma casa portuguesa" makes our village come alive again,
in a song. Remember? There was fresh rosemary growing
outside our door. Down the *rua*, that woman with the rich
cousin in Brasil…

ANTÓNIO
  I remember her.

ROSIDA
  She had roses in her garden. The church had blue tiles. The
  women would get together to bake bread. Do you remember
  that aroma?

ANTÓNIO
  Yes, Rosida –

ROSIDA
  "Uma casa portuguesa" isn't fascist. It's lovely!

ANTÓNIO
  That's what makes it good propaganda. It says poverty is a
  virtue. (*to his bandmates*) A virtue. (*back to* ROSIDA) Are
  there more hateful words?

ROSIDA
  "Blessed are the poor, for theirs is the kingdom of heaven."

ANTÓNIO
  But on earth, Rosida, some profit while others starve.

ROSIDA
  What does that have to do with a pretty song?

ANTÓNIO
  Rosida, they made us play that song over and over. If you
  listen, you will hear the voice of Salazar, telling us how to be
  Portuguese.

ROSIDA
  A song is a song. You made my daughter think I'm a fascist.

41

ANTÓNIO
  Are you?

ROSIDA
  I don't know. António. I was young when I left. I only
  know what they taught us in school. The glory of Portugal.
  We discovered the world. It *was* nice back then, wasn't it?
  In our village. Don't you remember?

ANTÓNIO
  No. I remember the secret police and the silence and the
  torture.

ROSIDA
  I don't remember that.

ANTÓNIO
  No. Because you left. You caught a husband and moved away.

ROSIDA
  I sacrificed everything I loved.

ANTÓNIO
  If you didn't want to leave, then why did you?

ROSIDA
  I wanted to give my daughter a better life.

LUISA
  Oh *mãe*!

ANTÓNIO
  And you have.

LUISA
  What is going on?

ROSIDA

(*coldly*) Thank you, *senhor* Silveira, for teaching my daughter. It has been lovely to see you again after so many years.

> *ROSIDA exits. ANTÓNIO is heartbroken.*
> *LUISA, shocked, turns to ANTÓNIO.*

ANTÓNIO

That's all for today, Luisa. Let's continue tomorrow.

> *LUISA nods, then runs after her mother.*

> *The rest of the BAND MEMBERS enter with*
> *AMÁLIA. They perform "Lavava no rio, lavava,"[6]*
> *a song about the preciousness of Amália*
> *Rodrigues's dreams, and how she shared them*
> *with her mother when she was young, poor, and*
> *learning to sing fado from the women doing*
> *laundry in her bairro. The song starts with the*
> *words "Lavava no rio, lavava / Gelava-me o*
> *frio, gelava ..." The musicians play with intimacy,*
> *happy to be together. ANTÓNIO is comforted by*
> *the presence of the ghost of AMÁLIA. They exit.*

Scene 7

As ruas

On the street. TRISTÃO *enters,*
followed by LUISA.

TRISTÃO
Do you feel the *fantasmas*?

LUISA
The ghosts?

TRISTÃO
Yes.

LUISA
Where are we?

TRISTÃO
The Mouraria.

LUISA
Where fado was born!

TRISTÃO
Yes. One of the oldest parts of Lisboa. So much history.
So much longing.

LUISA
It's like a labyrinth echoing. A shell. The voices, fighting,
loving, telling the news of the day. Like in your poems
tonight. I loved it. Your voice. So much feeling.

44

TRISTÃO
Muito obrigada.

LUISA
That line about *ruas* being *voltinhas*… The streets are like the winding notes of fado. You can get lost so easily.

TRISTÃO
Do you love getting lost? I do.

LUISA
Yes. The city is so sensual. I love the roughness of the old stones. The walls… touching them awakens… They're like the skin of the city. But I'm still outside the body.

TRISTÃO
We're here. Maria Severa's house.

LUISA
The woman who invented fado?

TRISTÃO
Yes. I had to bring you here.

LUISA
Oh Tristão! (*reading the plaque in front of the house*) "Her father was a gypsy…" – Tristão, that should be "Roma" – "her mother, a famous prostitute…" – that should be "sex worker." Not a very enlightened plaque.

TRISTÃO
She had a hard life.

LUISA
(*still reading*) They ran a tavern, here? Oh. This is where Severa sang! The Count of Vimioso fell in love with her. But

then he cast her off. She died, at twenty-six, of tuberculosis. Oh, so sad.

TRISTÃO
The poets who knew Severa back in her day said she was generous, that she had fire in her eyes. That her guitar was her constant companion. Severa loved the Count so much that she invented fado for him. He honored her by laying a beautiful black shawl on her sexy shoulders.

LUISA
So romantic.

TRISTÃO
Luisa, now, you feel a bit more inside the skin of the city? You can feel its heart, beating?

LUISA nods, overcome with feeling.

TRISTÃO
Now, all *fadistas* honour Severa by wearing the shawl. (*pulling out a shawl*) May I?

LUISA nods and TRISTÃO puts the shawl on her.

LUISA
Muito obrigada.

TRISTÃO
De nada.

> *LUISA resumes singing Amália Rodrigues's "Barco negro (Mãe Preta)," starting with the words "De manhã, que medo, que me achasses feia! ..."*

TRISTÃO
"Barco negro." A glorious fado.

> LUISA *sings the last line of the song's first*
> *verse.* TRISTÃO *moves closer to her.*

TRISTÃO
He shows her how enchanting she is when they lie together
on the sand.

> *They kiss.*

Scene 8

A fundação

Outside AMÁLIA's house. ROSIDA is
waiting, impatiently. AMÁLIA and RUI are
sitting together, whispering intimately.

LUISA enters, in a cloud of romance,
happily wrapped in her shawl.

ROSIDA

Your cousin is waiting. Where were you?

LUISA's mood quickly changes to defiance.

LUISA

My father was a good man. He didn't deserve to live his
whole life with someone who didn't love him.

ROSIDA

What are you talking about?

LUISA

What's going on? With you and António? Did you love
Dad at all?

ROSIDA

It was different then. Your father came looking for a wife.
I didn't know him. Everything was very formal. Women had
to stay in the house, look down from our windows. Men had
to talk to us from the street.

48

LUISA
That's like *Romeo and Juliet*!

ROSIDA
It wasn't. At least not for me. We hardly got to talk. But I knew if I wanted a family, I needed a better life. And *querida*, your father and I, when we set up our home, for you, we fell in love. You made our lives make sense.

LUISA
Excuses.

ROSIDA
I grew up with António. He was my first kiss. The heart, *querida*, it's a mess. One day, you will see. *A verdade é clara; a mentira, sombra.*

LUISA
You're the one who is keeping the truth in the dark.

ROSIDA
Shh, here comes your cousin.

LUISA
Okay, but we're not done.

RUI
Tia! Here for your tour?

ROSIDA
Yes!

ROSIDA
Luisa, we are in her house!

> *AMÁLIA smiles. It is her pleasure to share her home with* ROSIDA *and* RUI.

RUI
Bem-vindas!

LUISA
(*looking around*) Wow. She was so devoted. To her music.
Her *guitarra*! Exquisite. Her piano. Her composers. They
must have worked with her. Right here. Her earrings, her
shoes, her makeup table… Everything is ready for her to go
on stage.

>   AMÁLIA *is pleased.*

RUI
She was devoted to her talent. We will always be
devoted to her.

>   AMÁLIA *gestures for* ROSIDA *to sit.* ROSIDA
>   *doesn't see* AMÁLIA, *but she sits.* AMÁLIA *wraps*
>   *her arm around* ROSIDA, *who is comforted.*

RUI
In her dining room, she entertained famous musicians,
writers, politicians. Here are the portraits artists made of her.

LUISA
And all these beautiful dresses.

RUI
Such beautiful dresses…

>   RUI *drapes one over himself, smiling.*
>   LUISA *snickers, but warns* RUI *with*
>   *her eyes about her mother.*

LUISA
Her shawl…

RUI

Yes. The shawl of the *fadista*. *Fadistas* learn to sing from their *madrinhas*, their godmothers of fado. Your *madrinha* is a more experienced *fadista*. She takes care of you as you practise, as you try, as you fail, as you try again. And when you can really sing, when you have fado in your soul, when you have become a *fadista*, your *madrinha*, she lays the shawl on your shoulders.

> *LUISA, moved, then embarrassed, realizes she's not a fadista yet. She slips her shawl off.*
>
> *But ROSIDA saw the bit with the dress.*

ROSIDA

Rui, we haven't met your wife, have we?

RUI

No, *tia*. I'm not married.

ROSIDA

You're not married?

LUISA

Mãe...

ROSIDA

(*to LUISA*) I don't mean to pry, of course.

RUI

Eu sou homossexual, tia. E uma drag queen também.

> *Silence.*

ROSIDA

My poor sister.

51

LUISA

Mãe! How dare you!

RUI

It's okay, *prima.*

ROSIDA

No wonder she stopped writing about you. She couldn't bear the shame.

LUISA

Stop it, right now.

ROSIDA

You killed my sister.

LUISA

Mom! Don't.

> *ROSIDA shakes her head, exits.*
> *RUI and LUISA alone.*

LUISA

Oh my god. Rui. I'm so sorry.

RUI

(*pensive… then deciding to tell LUISA his story*) One day, I heard my mother playing her Amália record. I snuck into her room, I took some jewelry, teased my hair up. From the living room, I could hear my mother singing "Estranha forma de vida" – "a strange way of life."[7] And then, in the mirror, I saw her: Amália. Amália looking back at me. I put on her lipstick. I created myself into something, someone, everyone could love: fascists, communists, everybody, the rich, the poor, no matter how hard their life was. Amália stood proud, let her voice free. *Estranha forma de vida.* Then I heard the record end, my mother's heels clicked, down the hall. I pulled one earring off, the other still dangling from my ear. When my mother saw me, she – she – her face closed. She turned away from me. I think, she thought – she'd failed. *Prima*, imagine living in a house where your mother won't say one word to you. And the village. They did anything to pretend I was straight. Everyone lied. I became a ghost, even to myself. I knew I had to go. But I never imagined my mother would die without ever speaking to me again.

The ghost of AMÁLIA *puts her shawl over* RUI's *shoulders, comforting him. Lights dim.*

Scene 9

O museu

AMÁLIA is frozen, as if she were an exhibit.

*ANTÓNIO and LUISA meet at the
Fado Museum (Museu do Fado).
Inside we hear recordings of the calls
of Portuguese street vendors.*

ANTÓNIO
Thank you for coming.

ROSIDA
António, is this even a museum?

ANTÓNIO
It's our new museum for fado. They want it to be creative.

ROSIDA
Why is it so dark?

ANTÓNIO
So we can focus on the sound.

ROSIDA
(*listening to the street vendors' calls*) What does this have to
do with fado?

ANTÓNIO
It's the calls of vendors. Amália was a lemon seller.

We hear the opening chords of Amália Rodrigues's "Abandono." [8]

ROSIDA
I thought a museum had things under glass.

ANTÓNIO
Not always.

We see a video projection of AMÁLIA singing "Abandono."

ROSIDA
Ai meu Deus. What now? A movie? With no sound?

ANTÓNIO
It's a recreation of the Tarrafal camp, in Cabo Verde. One of the dictatorship's worst prisons. With Amália singing "Abandono." The fado about her lover being locked up, for free speech. It was censored.

ROSIDA
I thought it was a love song.

ANTÓNIO
It is.

Amália's BAND enters and they perform "Abandono." AMÁLIA sings, starting with the words "Por teu livre pensamento / Foram-te longe encerrar ..." Light from the projector falls across ANTÓNIO and ROSIDA's faces. ROSIDA's heart slowly starts to open, until she is weeping openly.

ROSIDA
(*covering her feelings*) But António, it was a soft dictatorship.

ANTÓNIO
Querida, what does that mean?

ROSIDA
He wasn't as bad as Hitler or Mussolini.

ANTÓNIO
Soft. Who told you this?

ROSIDA
My older sister. My parents. May they rest in peace. It was a soft dictatorship.

ANTÓNIO
There is no soft dictatorship. Think about the lyrics. Listen.

ROSIDA
Amália said it was just a love song.

ANTÓNIO
You don't think that was her way of…

ROSIDA
António, don't be so hard on Salazar. He was like a father to the Portuguese. He was a good Catholic.

ANTÓNIO
Why are you defending him?

ROSIDA
I – it's what people said. When I was a girl.

ANTÓNIO
I know. When you left, you were only eighteen.

*ROSIDA starts to cry. She quietly sings
the first lines of "Abandono," first in
Portuguese, then, meditatively, in English.*

ANTÓNIO
So far, my words cannot reach you.

ROSIDA
You hear only the wind... only the sea. Why am I crying?

ANTÓNIO embraces ROSIDA.

ANTÓNIO
You feel for her, for her lover locked up. It is that feeling that
saves us.

ROSIDA
I'm locked up. I've been locked up.

*She searches his face, finds
understanding. They kiss.*

Scene 10

A andorinha

TRISTÃO and LUISA are in bed together.
He wraps the shawl around her, but she
shakes her head and slips it off. He nods, puts
it around her again. She smiles tentatively
and allows it to stay on her shoulders.

TRISTÃO
I have something for you, my *fadista*.

He hands her a piece of foolscap filled with
handwriting. It's a poem he wrote for her.

LUISA
Oh Tristão.

(*reading*)

"For Luisa.
Like *andorinhas* they swoop over Lisbon
returning in summer
the ones we exported
we were starving for books and bread
we traded our families for hope
Empire made you
a foreigner

but you've remade yourself
into one of us
what is fado
but a listening to the silence
a tuning into your place among the others."

I love it. I'm honoured.

TRISTÃO
But what?

LUISA
I'm not sure I've tuned into my place, but I'm trying.

TRISTÃO
Oh Luisinha, you will.

> *They kiss.*

LUISA
Oh, Tristão –

TRISTÃO
Yes?

LUISA
I want to be with you.

TRISTÃO
(*patronizingly*) Oh Luisa.

LUISA
I want to stay here, in Portugal, with you.

TRISTÃO
But... could you?... How?

LUISA
We'd find a way. I've never felt like this.

He kisses her. She kisses back, hungrily.

TRISTÃO
You're so beautiful. You inspire me so much. (*more to himself than to LUISA*) I write all night.

LUISA
(*kissing him again*) I can't bear to be apart. Not even for a moment.

TRISTÃO
Ah, Luisinha, my beautiful muse. I must –

TRISTÃO gets up and starts to get dressed, a ring falls out of his pocket. LUISA picks it up.

LUISA
You dropped something.

TRISTÃO
Ah – I...

LUISA
Why do you have a ring in your pocket?

TRISTÃO
I can explain –

LUISA
You're married?

TRISTÃO
It's *complicado.*

LUISA
Get out.

> *He doesn't move. Instead, she dresses herself frantically. She takes off the shawl, throws it at him, then exits.*

Scene 11

Inúteis

ANTÓNIO and his BAND are playing. The ghost of AMÁLIA enters and sings "Acho inúteis as palavras" ("I find words useless").[9]

LUISA enters and cuts off the end of the song, much to ANTÓNIO's annoyance.

LUISA
Mestre Silveira?

ANTÓNIO
Luisa!

LUISA
What a great fado. *Words, eyes, bodies, my gestures are useless, to speak to you of love.* You play it so well.

ANTÓNIO
Thank you. Luisa, it's good to see you. I want you to know I have the utmost respect for the memory of your father.

LUISA
Yeah. Don't worry about it. I know. Love's a mess.

ANTÓNIO
I see.

LUISA
Senhor Silveira, I understand now. Fado is a way of being. It's the streets, it's the crimes of your country, it's the longing for home, it's missing the dead, it's heartbreak.

ANTÓNIO
Luisa, you can have all the heartbreak in the world, but I am
sorry, you're just not Portuguese enough.

LUISA
Maybe there is no home. For any of us. There is no Portugal.
No Canada. There is no you. No me. No fate.

ANTÓNIO
Luisa, fado means fate. Fado binds us to each other. Fado
is the courage to love, even though there is heartbreak;
the courage to sing of life, even though there is death. I'm
sorry this cord has been broken for you. I don't know who I
would be without our music, without my culture.

LUISA
Let me sing.

ANTÓNIO
Luisa, no.

LUISA
Who are you to judge? You sit there and decide who's
Portuguese? Who's not? I don't need to be born here to
have soul!

ANTÓNIO
Luisa, I'm afraid you do.

LUISA is devastated.

ANTÓNIO
(*gently*) I've given you what I can.

LUISA exits, heartbroken.

Scene 12

Estranha forma de vida

*Inside Lisbon's Finalmente Drag Club,
decorated with silver glittery arches, mirrors,
neon. LUISA enters and sits at a table,
heartbroken. RUI enters as AMALIANA,
in full drag. She sings "Estranha forma
de vida" ("A strange way of life").*

*AMALIANA's rendition of the song is beautiful
and heartfelt. She finishes triumphantly, sweeps
forward for a bow. LUISA applauds. AMALIANA
is surprised and delighted to see LUISA.*

Scene 13

Fado

ANTÓNIO and ROSIDA, in their old village.

ROSIDA
Why did they destroy those houses? That was a lovely street.

ANTÓNIO
They want to put in condominiums.

ROSIDA
Why am I here? I don't know anyone anymore.

ANTÓNIO
You know me. I still have the family house.

ROSIDA
My sister sold ours.

ANTÓNIO
A pity.

ROSIDA
Why did they pull out the olive trees? They were hundreds
of years old. The olives had such a particular flavour. One
I've never found anywhere else.

ANTÓNIO
The European Union told us to plant corn. Then they
realized corn is grown everywhere. So. Do you see? There?
That's where we're trying to replant the olive trees.

ROSIDA
They're so small.

ANTÓNIO
You have to start somewhere. Rosida, you know, I can still feel our old village.

ROSIDA
How?

ANTÓNIO
I don't know, I still feel them. The people. Do you remember *senhor* Costa? He used to live over there.

ROSIDA
Oh yes, he'd give us those little butterscotch candies.

ANTÓNIO
From his relatives in America.

ROSIDA
He was so shy and kind. What happened to him?

ANTÓNIO
They took him. The secret police. They said he was a communist. We never saw him again. Some say they threw him in the river. I started asking questions, too many questions, dangerous questions. My father handed me his *guitarra* and said, son, put your questions, your feelings into this. That's why I started playing *guitarra*.

ROSIDA
I remember your father's playing. He was so good.

ANTÓNIO
My father had to work, keep his job, keep his mouth shut. All around us buildings were crumbling. Perhaps it is our

curse, he said, to have built this empire and to watch it decay from within. My father helped build new buildings for Salazar. All clean lines. Purity. So my father, he showed me some chords, patted me on the shoulder as if he were shoving me off to sea. He was. I went to the neighbourhood *tasca*. I had to learn from others, the men at the club. But you know, my father was proud when I got my first professional card, even if it was from the government. I played for them, you know. I played for everybody. PIDE,[10] the secret police, the communists, the capitalists, the fascists. But by then, my feelings were so driven down. The strings of my guitar held them for me. It was terrible, you know. Not trusting anyone. Keeping silent. Knowing you are keeping silent because you are afraid. We stood like we were brave, proud. But inside, we blamed ourselves.

ROSIDA

Oh *querido*. For what?

ANTÓNIO

Being cowards. It's all there, in the fado, if you know how to listen. My father said Salazar forbid fado. But as the *Estado Novo*[11] wore on, someone began to see people needed something to be proud of, somewhere to express emotion. So we put our feelings there and did nothing.

ROSIDA

I feel like those olive trees. The small ones, the new ones. Like the deep things are all pulled out and I have to start all over.

ANTÓNIO

Oh, *querida*. Poverty made us export our own peasants – like you. (*pause*) Rosida, would you stay? Even if we've cut down the olive trees? We could start over together.

ROSIDA
Here?

ANTÓNIO
Yes.

ROSIDA
Oh, *querido*...

ANTÓNIO
My life is simple. I can't offer you much.

ROSIDA
That doesn't matter.

ANTÓNIO
Remember that guy I was when I rode that bicycle for you, back in the town hall? I'm almost as strong.

       ROSIDA laughs.

ANTÓNIO
Say yes.

ROSIDA
Oh António, I don't belong here anymore.

ANTÓNIO
You do.

ROSIDA
No, I don't. I will always love you. But I made my life in Canada, with Luisa. I'm sorry.

      She touches him softly on the cheek, then exits.

Scene 14

Tristão

TRISTÃO enters all alone. He sits down
on his bench. He arranges his things, takes
out his book and his pen, and looks like
he's about to write a poem. He can't.
He stuffs his book back in his bag.

Scene 15

Tudo isto existe

*LUISA goes to RUI after his
performance as an AMALIANA. Nearby,
AMÁLIA watches over them.*

LUISA
You were magnificent.

RUI
Obrigado, prima.

LUISA
I feel so lost. Why do I feel so lost?

RUI
Prima... we are all lost.

LUISA
I don't belong anywhere. I have no home. Like a boat at sea,
unmoored.

RUI
There is no home. There is only the sea. But we sing anyway.
This, this, *prima*, this is fado. This is what Amália said...

> *He recites the last line from the chorus
> of Amália Rodrigues's "Tudo isto é
> fado" ("All of this is fado")*[12]*:*

"All this exists, all this is sad, all this is fado."

And all that is in you, *querida*. (*pause*) It's time, *prima*.

> RUI *and* AMÁLIA *motion* LUISA *to the stage.*
> *They escort her there.* LUISA *sings "Grito,"*
> *starting with "Silêncio! ..." echoing the first*
> *song of the play, but with a unique feeling, all*
> *her own. Suddenly,* LUISA *bursts forward*
> *with enormous talent and passion, which*
> *carries her through the song.* TRISTÃO *and*
> ROSIDA *slip in quietly, sit at separate tables,*
> *in the dark, heartbroken, listening. Before the*
> *final chorus,* ANTÓNIO *and* ROSIDA *gaze*
> *at each other – maybe they can try again.*

> *Swept up by the power of the song,* RUI *and*
> AMÁLIA *join in for the final chorus.* RUI
> *and* AMÁLIA *lovingly place the classic black*
> *shawl, in honour of Severa, on* LUISA*'s*
> *shoulders.* LUISA *smiles through her tears.*
> *She knows that she is, at last, a fadista.*

THE END

Afterword

Mercedes Bátiz-Benét

Every language has a few words that its native speakers say are untranslatable. You can learn a lot about a culture by examining those words, which must express something both particular and fundamental about the culture to be singled out in this way. I find it fascinating how often these essential words describe a variety of sorrow – the Czechs have *lítost*, with apparently a peculiarly Czech air of regret, whereas the Russians have тоскá (*toská*), with a whiff of the gaping spiritual steppes; the Americans have *the blues*, oppression masquerading as a mood, the Japanese 物の哀れ (*mono no aware*), similar perhaps to Virgil's *lacrimae rerum* in the *Aeneid*; and on and on. Perhaps this puzzling intersection between unhappiness and the failure of communication can be explained: we don't feel understood when we're heartbroken; we feel unique, alone, forgotten. There is surely a vast catalogue of sub-sadnesses, shades and variations to be perused, but the Portuguese version, *saudade*, is probably the most famous. It communicates a longing for home when far away at sea, a yearning for something you may not have even ever had, that only the Portuguese know, and therefore only the Portuguese have a special word for it.

I am from Mexico, which has known its share of miseries, but they are Mexican miseries, and I can never fully inhabit the lived experience of the Portuguese, nor the particular sources of their tears. In directing the premiere production of Elaine's wonderful play, however, I had to rely on a certain article of faith: that sorrow *can* be translated.

There is some basis for mutual understanding, I believe. The way I see it, this play is about more than what it means to be Portuguese; it is about what it means to emigrate, to leave your homeland, your language, your traditions, your family, the bones of your ancestors, the sounds and smells of your childhood – to begin a new life somewhere else, always wondering if you should never have left. These emotions are their own homeland. I am a citizen of Diaspora, just like Elaine, and just like the characters in *Fado*, and that means, on some important level, that we do speak the same language.

But, as Elaine puts it, *Fado* is the immigrant's story in reverse. The hero of the play is returning, not arriving. The fact that Luisa is searching for home in a place she knows only as an abstraction struck me deeply. My son, like the play's protagonist, will grow up in Canada with his mother's homeland as a defining but distant part of his identity. He won't know it the way I do, and may not know it at all, and so I admit a part of my faith in translatability could be wishful thinking: I want my son and I to understand each other, even though we are from different countries, and do not even share the same mother tongue.

My son will grow up in a safe country; but in a sense, like Luisa, he will wonder where he's really from, because rootlessness is the settler Canadian condition. I sometimes wonder whether I have sacrificed something that his soul will need for the sake of safety, and I believe there should be a word for that particular sorrow, known perhaps only to immigrant mothers.

And yet there's something about sorrow that feels like it doesn't fit into words at all. I felt a deep connection to the themes and characters in *Fado* and believed I could bring life to the words, but there was a third element that bound the whole piece together: fado music itself, suffused with an anguish that is almost preverbal, too ancient to stay contained, a species of speech closer to a moan or a shriek than to mere syllables and consonants.

So, when I discovered that there was a world-class fado singer living on Vancouver Island, choosing to produce and direct this play became truly inevitable. The singer's name is Sara Marreiros, and becoming friends with her has been one of the great gifts of my artistic career and of my life. Sara's daughter, too, was born here in Canada, and so we found an immediate and common vocabulary. Sara came on board as musical director, which was invaluable, but most importantly she performed in the show *Fado* itself, as the ghost of the Queen of Fado, Amália Rodrigues.

There is another kind of untranslatability: you cannot achieve mastery of a form through speaking. It must be lived, but once achieved, it is undeniable. If any of us had any doubts about the universality of human suffering, they were erased in the opening moments of the play: the curtains part, and there stands Sara, who delivers the first notes of the famous fado song "Grito," and its first word: *Silêncio*. Oddly enough, "Grito's" first word is the negation of words. Does it mean, "Shut up and listen"? Or is it an ode to silence? And then: "*Do silêncio faço um grito ...*" – "Out of the silence, I make a scream ..."

The audience was invariably and immediately captivated. Whether they were Portuguese or not, they understood the raw emotion. Our grief goes deeper than individual circumstances; it is human, cosmic, eternal. It is time, and distance, and rhythm and melody, the beginning and the end. It is so much more than solitude. It is what binds us all. That, perhaps, is what "Fado," both the music and the play, is all about.

TOP: Luisa (Natércia Napoleão) begins to believe in her love for Tristão (Chris Perrins) and her abilities as a fado singer, and serenades Tristão with the lyrics in the beautiful love song "Barco negro (Mãe Preta)." (Photo: Derek Ford)

BOTTOM: As the Ghost of Amália (Sara Marreiros) looks on, Rui (Pedro M. Siqueira) confides in Luisa (Natércia Napoleão), telling her about the first day he dressed in drag, as Amaliana, and his subsequent rejection by his small village. (Photo: Derek Ford)

Four Amálias: Voicing Drag

Lila Ellen Gray

A January evening, midnight, 2003. The club is in a zone of Lisbon informally known as the *docas* (docks), which in the early 2000s, was a relatively new area for nightlife. Discos, large franchise restaurants, and nightclubs line up along the river leading out of the city proper. I arrive with a friend at an address off a narrow, dark side street. I am carrying my tripod and a camera case. The bouncer, a large man guarding the entrance, looks at me suspiciously and asks who I am. I give him the name of the producer who invited me. The doors open to a dark, intimate space, a small stage with four rows of folding chairs set up in front of it, a dance floor, swirling colors of disco ball lights, clouds of cigarette smoke, and recorded dance music booming. Gay men in their twenties and thirties sit and stand along the bar, cruising; various kinds of negotiations for sex appear to be under way. My friend points to audience members whose faces she recognizes from television.

"The Show Must Go On" features numerous scantily clad drag beauties, lip-syncing sequences to the voices of female stars, framed by two prominently muscled men who, the program informs, are among Portugal's most "prestigious male strippers."[13] A svelte drag queen wearing a bobbed brunette wig, a plunging bikini top, a choker around her neck, and a tattoo around her upper arm, who does not resemble Amália at any stage in her career, lip-syncs to an Amália recording of the first verse of "Foi Deus" (It Was God [who gave this voice to me]), gesturing expressively with her arms and hands: "I don't know, no one knows / Why I sing the fado in this sorrow-filled key of pain and weeping."[14] At the end of the first verse, as the recorded instrumentalists strum, she turns her back to the audience and, with hips swaying, walks back to join the strippers, who are lip-syncing voices of crowd members yelling "Amália! Amália!" This first Amália remains with her back to the audience, positioned between the two men.

A second Amália enters to loud applause. She has pinned-up blonde curly hair and wears a tight sleeveless dress. She stands at the right of the stage, taking up the third verse by mouthing the words and "singing" out to the audience with her body. As she launches into the final verse, "It was God / Who gave voice to the wind / Light to the heavens / And who gave blue to the waves to the sea," the playback abruptly stops, interrupted by a third Amália – a brunette in a slinky silver dress. She moves her lips to what sounds like Amália's speaking voice in old age with the resonant acoustics of a live performance in a large hall. "I have so many saudades, saudades for my voice," she says. We then hear the sound of Amália's voice at the end of her career – guttural, raspy, and deep – singing the words to "Foi Deus" lip-synced by the drag queen. The other two Amálias pick up the words in the last verse and alternate, sometimes appearing to sing at the same time to a soundtrack of a younger Amália, and sometimes joined by the strippers. These two Amálias stop before singing the final line: "*Ai*, and he [God] gave this voice to me." Then they exit the stage.

Amália number three launches into a performance of the Amália standard, "Lágrima" (Tear). The stage lights dim, and "Lágrima" is cut short. We hear the recorded sound of the guitarra and viola playing the introduction to "Estranha Forma de Vida" (Strange Form of Life), a tour de force of Amália's repertoire. Amália number three stands with arms outstretched while another drag queen walks out from the stage door and takes her place, back to the audience, directly behind her, arms also outstretched. Amália number three exits, and as the instrumental introduction continues, a full-blown diva Amália late in her career is revealed standing in a characteristic opening-of-the-show pose: back to audience, right arm outstretched, as if in invitation. She is the only Amália of the evening who actually resembles Amália Rodrigues in appearance. She wears a wig the color and style of Amália's hair when she was in her sixties (reddish tinged, big around her face); she wears the fadista's black shawl, immense dangling earrings, a large silver brooch, and a ring with a large stone. Beneath the shawl this "Ur-Amália" is wrapped in a dress in the colors of the Portuguese flag. She turns to face the audience, keeping her right arm outstretched in Amália fashion, throws back her head, closes her eyes, and starts to sing. Rather than placing her left hand on her heart (where Amália's would have been), she cups her left breast, jutting it outward. As she sings, her hands mimic common gestures of a female fadista – furling, unfurling, clasped in front of her as in a position of prayer. When she mouths the word "saudade" in the first verse, she emphasizes it with a side-to-side inflection of her head. Then at the end of the verse, she signals to the (absent) instrumentalists with her right hand. Her eyes remain closed, and she sings (lip-syncs) the entire fado without interruption, the precise movements of her mouth led by the words, sounds, and inflections of Amália's voice in its prime resounding.

Through the magnified lens of drag, this spectacle calls atten-tion to performative details (as all drag does) in which the style's meaning[15] reveals a feminine that is specifically embodied and particularly sexualized. The female body in stylized detail is made visible in the sway of a pair of hips, revealing clothing, a cupped or accentuated breast, the feminine made more "real" precisely through its "made-up-ness." The melodramatic performance of fado is indexed by the pantomime of the face expressing stylized emotion, and fado performance in its feminized version is refer-enced not only by the "female" body and by costume but also by the sweeping or intimate hand and arm gestures used by Amália or by female fadistas. The feminine is set up against, and framed by, the hyper-masculinity of the strippers, who are a constant presence on stage.

This performance by the four "Amálias" presents multiple ways of experiencing, embodying, and imagining Amália and is thus in keeping with the discourse of fans regarding her capacity for dramatic and musical transformation and newness: *Every time I listen to Amália, I hear something new. She had this remarkable capability to transform herself.* Or, as the Amaliano Fernando told me, "I found all of these women in her."[16] The genre of camp provides a frame that invites the "troubling"[17] of tropes of gender, sexuality, and nation as they are commonly construed and bound together in Amália and fado mythology. The enactment of Amália's multiplicity in this context becomes a "space of ambivalence," with fado's illicit history implicitly granting "room to maneuver."[18] Sonorously, multiplicity is rendered by using recordings of the same fado from different moments of Amália's career in playback, foregrounding different timbres of her voice.

Silently singing along is common in amateur fado listening practice (see chapter 1 of *Fado Resounding*). The lip-syncing in this performance by cross-dressed Amálias might be understood as a fully embodied extension of this practice, in which the expressive play of the "passing" body becomes a conduit for the interiorization of the voice of Amália. With the voice of the individual actor rendered mute in this act of ventriloquism, the body becomes all voice, all hearing, the act of miming the substituted voice demanding a heightened listening of the performer. The final Amália performs the ultimate exteriorization of the interiorized voice or hearing. "She" "sings" with eyes closed and head thrown back (two icons of interiority and soulfulness in fado); she uses exaggerated hand and arm gestures. In cupping her left breast with her right hand, particularly on the word *coração* (heart), a gesture of soulfulness (putting the hand to the heart) is inflected in an act of inventive "signifying"[19] such that soulfulness in rendering fado, of embodying Amália, is explicitly feminized and sexualized. Finally, through hyperbolic performative excess and parody, this performance calls attention to the nation – feminine complex that haunts both fado and the Amália phenomenon, destabilizing it by rendering it visible. Through her costume of Portuguese flag dress, this ultra-feminized "Ur-Amália" is linked through a gesture that camp renders satire to the soulful "voice of Portugal."

From "Haunted by a Throat of Silver," in *Fado Resounding: Affective Politics and Urban Life*, Lila Ellen Gray, pp. 179–226. Copyright 2013, Duke University Press. All rights reserved. Republished by permission of the copyright holder. www.dukeupress.edu.

Endnotes

Fado: The Saddest Music in the World

1 "Silence! / Of the silence I make a cry ..." The song "Grito," composed by Amália Rodrigues and Carlos Gonçalves, can be found on Amália Rodrigues's 1983 album *Lágrima* (Columbia Records).

2 "In a Portuguese home it's good / Bread and wine on the table ..." See track one on the 2012 compilation *Uma casa portuguesa* (Vinyl Passion), or, for a live recording, see *Amalia à l'Olympia* (Columbia Records, 1958). "Uma casa portuguesa" was composed in 1952 by Artur Vaz da Fonseca, Reinaldo Ferreira, and Vasco Matos Sequeira.

3 One of the oldest viewpoints in Lisbon, a terrace with a panoramic view of the castle and the city centre, literally "the mirador of grace."

4 See Afonso's 1973 album of the same name (label Orfeu).

5 "I know, my love, / That you never started to depart ..." "Barco negro (Mãe Preta)" was composed in 1955 by Caco Velho (Mateus Nunes), David Mourão-Ferreira, and Piratini (Antônio Amábile).

6 Composed by Amália Rodrigues and Fontes Rocha, track one on the 1980 album *Gostava de ser quem era* ("I would like to be who I was") (Columbia Records / EMI).

7 Composed by Alfredo Duarte and Amália Rodrigues. See track fourteen on the 1985 compilation *O melhor de Amália (Estranha forma de vida)* (Columbia Records) or track nine on *The Art of Amália Rodrigues* (Hemisphere / EMI, 1998).

8 Composed by Alain Oulman and David Mourão-Ferreira. See track six on the 1962 album *Amália Rodrigues* (Columbia Records).

9 Composed by António Sousa Freitas and José Joaquim Cavalheiro Jr. See track two on the album *Amália 1963* (Ducretet Thomson, 1963).

10 Polícia Internacional e de Defesa do Estado (International and State Defense Police).

11 The "New State," or Second Republic of Portugal (1933–1974), one of the longest dictatorships in modern times.

12 Composed by Aníbal Nazaré and Fernando de Carvalho. See track five on the 1965 compilation *Portugal's Great Amália Rodrigues* (Monitor Records) or, for a live recording, see track five on *Amalia à l'Olympia* (Columbia Records, 1958).

13   "The Show Must Go On" was written and directed by Carlos Castro.

14   "Foi Deus," lyrics and music by Alberto Janes.

15   Dick Hebdige, *Subculture: The Meaning of Style* (London: Routledge, 1979).

16   For a discussion of how the concept of transformation works in relation to divas with large gay followings (here with reference to Maria Callas), see Wayne Koestenbaum, *The Queen's Throat: Opera, Homosexuality, and the Mystery of Desire* (New York: Poseidon, 1993), 139, 145: "Careers with gay followings often have moments of rupture and reinvention: moments when the star's body or persona radically shifts and proves the former self to have been a fabrication. The gay fan, schooled in the gap between public manner and private feeling, may identify less with Callas' newfound glamour than with her former plainness; or he may identify with the *rift between the two* ... We love her because she incarnated vocal multiplicity and heterogeneity" (emphasis added).

17   Judith Butler, *Gender Trouble* (New York: Routledge, 1990).

18   I agree with Judith Butler that "there is no necessary relation between drag and subversion ... [Drag] may well be used in the service of both the denaturalization and reidealization of hyperbolic heterosexual gender norms" (*Bodies That Matter: On the Discursive Limits of "Sex"* [New York: Routledge, 1993], 125).

19   Henry Louis Gates, *The Signifying Monkey* (New York: Oxford University Press, 1988).

Glossary

of Portuguese Words, Expressions, and Quotations Used in *Fado*

a andorinha – the swallow
Abandono – Abandonment
Acho inúteis as palavras – I find words useless
a fundaçao – the foundation
Ai! – Oh!
Ai meu Deus – Alas, my God
Ai, Santa Catarina. Luísa Margarida! – Alas, Saint Catherine. Luísa
    Margarida! (exaltation of the town's patron saint)
alegria da pobreza – the joy of poverty
andorinhas – swallows
as ruas – the streets
a tasca – the tavern
Até amanhã – See you tomorrow
A verdade é clara; a mentira, sombra – The truth is clear; a lie, dark
Barco negro (Mãe Preta) – Black boat (Black Mother)
Bem-vindas! – Welcome!
Bom dia! – Good morning!
Cafés? Pastéis de nata? – Coffees? Egg tarts?
caneca de viagem – travel mug
chouriço – sausage
complicado – complicated
coração – heart
De manhã, que medo, que me achasses feia! … – In the morning, such fear,
    that you would find me ugly! …
De nada – You're welcome
docas – docks
dois braços – two arms
duas princesas do Canadá – two princesses from Canada
Estranha forma de vida – A strange way of life
Eu sei, meu amor, / Que nem chegaste a partir … – I know, my love, / That
    you never started to depart …
Eu sou homossexual, tia. E uma drag queen também – I'm gay, Aunt. And
    also a drag queen
É um luxo – It's a luxury

fadista – fado singer (of any gender)

fado – (literally) fate

Fala português? – Speak Portuguese?

fantasmas – ghosts

Foi Deus – It was God

Fundação Amália Rodrigues, Casa Museu – Amália Rodrigues Foundation and House Museum

Gostava de ser quem era – I would like to be who I was

grito – a cry, scream, or call

guitarra (portuguesa) – (Portuguese) guitar

inúteis – useless

já não voltam – (they) won't/don't come back

lágrima – a tear

Lavava no rio, lavava / Gelava-me o frio, gelava ... – I washed in the river, I washed / The cold froze me, it froze me ...

limonada – lemonade

Lisboa – Lisbon

madrinha – godmother

mãe – mother

mais ou menos – more or less

maneira de ser – way of being

mestre – master

miradouro – viewpoint, mirador

Miradouro da Graça – (literally) mirador of grace

muito obrigada – thank you

Muito prazer – Pleasure to meet you

Museu do Fado – Fado Museum (Lisbon, Portugal)

No, querida – No, honey

Numa casa portuguesa fica bem / Pão e vinho sobre a mesa ... – In a Portuguese home it's good / Bread and wine on the table ...

obrigada – thanks

Obrigado, prima – Thank you, Cousin

Obrigado, tia – Thank you, Aunt

O fado não se aprende. O fado não se explica. O fado é uma maneira de ser – The fado cannot be learned. The fado cannot be explained. The fado is a manner (or way) of being

o melhor – the best

o museu – the museum

os sapatos – the shoes

o/um ferro a vapor – the/a steam iron

pão – bread

pastéis – pastries

Polícia Internacional e de Defesa do Estado (PIDE) – International and State Defense Police

Por favor. Eu quero um ferro a vapor, senhor – Please. I want a steam iron, sir

Por teu livre pensamento / Foram-te longe encerrar ... – For your free
thought / They locked you up far away ...

por três dias – for three days

Prazer – (It's a) pleasure

prima – cousin

queijo – cheese

querida – dear (fem.)

Querida, a roupa suja lava-se em casa! – Dear, don't air your dirty laundry
in public!

querido – dear (masc.)

redes – net, mesh, network, grid

Revolução dos Cravos – the Carnation Revolution (April 1974 military coup
in Lisbon, Portugal, which overthrew the Estado Novo regime, or "Second Republic")

rua – street

saudade – nostalgia, feeling of missing

senhor – mister

sentimento – feeling

Silêncio! / Do silêncio faço um grito ... – Silence! / Out of silence I make a
scream ...

sim – yes

tasca – tavern

tia – aunt

Tudo iste existe – All of this exists

Tudo isto é fado – All of this is fado

uma casa portuguesa – a Portuguese house

uma vergonha – a shame

vinho verde – green wine

Você é de Lisboa? – Are you from Lisbon?

voltinhas – little twists and turns

Further Reading, Viewing, and Listening

Author's Note: This list is incomplete, for fado is vast. The references below stem from my particular journey through fado. If your local community has a fado artist, seek them out, hear them live, buy their tunes!

Books

Gray, Lila Ellen. *Fado Resounding: Affective Politics and Urban Life*. Durham, NC: Duke University Press, 2013.

Holton, Kimberly DaCosta. "Bearing Material Witness to Musical Sound: Fado's L94 Museum Debut." Special issue, "Portuguese Cultural Studies," edited by Hilary Owen and Paulo de Medeiros. *Luso-Brazilian Review* 39, no. 2 (Winter 2002): 107–123.

Nery, Rui Viera. *A History of Portuguese Fado*. Translated by David Cranmer. Biblioteca do fado series. Lisbon, Portugal: Imprensa Nacional–Casa da Moeda, 2012. Simultaneously published in Portuguese as *Para uma história do fado* by the same publisher.

Rodrigues, Amália. *Versos*. Lisboa, Portugal: Cotovia, 2018 [1997] (no English translation).

Documentaries

Almeida, Bruno de. *The Art of Amália*. Arco Films, EMI Música Portugal, and Valentim de Carvalho Televisão, 2000. 90 min.

Broughton, Simon. *Mariza and the Story of Fado*. BBC. On DVD included with: Mariza, *Concerto em Lisboa*, EMI 50999 9 58857 2 8, 2013, compact disc. Also on YouTube, "Mariza and the Story of Fado (Full Documentary)," uploaded by we2 Productions, October 15, 2019, www.youtu.be /a5O6E59dV8Y. 60 min.

Caduff, Reto. *Charlie Haden: Rambling Boy*. PiXiu Films, 2008. 86 min. vimeo.com/ondemand/charliehadenramblingboy.

Pais, Ricardo. *Cabelo branco é saudade*. Promo Music, 2005. 85 min.

Saura, Carlos. *Fados.* Duvideo, Fado Filmes, and Zebra Producciones, 2007. 93 min. Also on YouTube, *"Fados* – Carlos Saura (1,280 × 720)," uploaded by Carlos Meireles, August 31, 2016, www.youtu.be/N3W_vVMUroI. 89 min.

Albums

Branco, Cristina. *Corpo iluminado.* Universal 981 469 0 and EmArcy 981 469 0, 2001.

——. *Murmúrios.* MW Records MWCD 4023, 1998.

Camané. *Uma noite de fados.* EMI–Valentim de Carvalho, 832905 2, 1995.

Carminho. *Canto.* Warner Music 2564619709, Warner Music Portugal 2564619709, and Parlophone 2564619709, 2014.

Carmo, Carlos do. *Nove fados e um cancão de amor.* Universal Music Portugal 066 874-2 and Mercury 066 874-2, 2002.

——. *Um homem na cidade.* Trova 6 330 900, 1977.

Cristo, Nuno. *Minha terra banzambira.* Independent release, 2005.

——. *Travels in Lusomania.* CD Baby BOOOGETYWU, 2005.

Deolinda, *Cancão ao Lado.* iPlay IP 1298 2, 2008.

Fé, Maria da. *Divino fado.* Companhia Nacional de Música CNM 101 CD, 2005.

Guerreiro, Katia. *Nas mãos do fado.* Ocarina OCA 007, 2003.

Haden, Charlie. *Charlie Haden Liberation Music Orchestra.* Probe SPB 1037, 1971.

——. *Closeness.* Horizon SP-710 and A&M Records SP-710, 1976.

Haden, Charlie, and Carlos Paredes. *Dialogues.* Polydor 843 445-2, 1990.

João, Gisela. *Gisela João.* Edições Valentim de Carvalho 0301-2, 2013.

Mariza. *Fado curvo.* EMI 7243 5 84237 2 3, 2003.

——. *Transparente.* World Connection 7243 4 77646 2 2 and Capitol Records 7243 4 77646 2 2, 2005.

Marreiros, Sara. *Minha luz (My Light).* Not On Label PM13812, 2006.

——. *Something Sweet on the Wind.* Independent release, 2012. saramarreiros .bandcamp.com.

Mísia. *Garras dos sentidos.* Detour 3984-22731-2, 1998.

——. *Ritual.* Erato 8573-85818-2, 2001.

Moura, Ana. *Desfado.* Universal Music Portugal 0602537205233 and Mercury 0602537205233, 2015.

——. *Para alem da saudade.* Universal Music Portugal 06025-1733898-2, 2007.

Rodrigues, Amália. *Amalia à l'Olympia.* Columbia Records FSX 123, 1957.

——. *Com que voz.* Columbia Records SPMX 5012, 1970.

——. *Fados Tradicionais.* Companhia Nacional de Música CNM 367CD, 2011.

——. *Folk Songs of Portugal*. Capitol Records DT 10438, 1966.

——. *Lisboa à noite*. Ducretet Thomson DEP 75070, 1958.

——. *Os maiores êxitos*. Tradisom, 2017.

Santos, Argentina. *Argentina Santos*. Companhia Nacional de Música CNM100CD, 2003.

Soares, Fernando Machado. *Portugal: Le fado de Coimbra*. Ocora C 582041, 2001.

Various artists. *Amália: Les voix du fado / As vozes do fado*. Universal Music France 4738157 and Decca 4738157, 2015.

Various artists. *Divas do fado novo*. Difference – Produção de Musíca DW5005CD, 2004.

Various artists. *Novo fado*. Different World DW50020CD, 2006.

Zambujo, António. *Guia*. Universal Music Portugal 00602537693030, 2014.

——. *Outro Sentido*. Universal Music Portugal 0602537713400, 2014.

——. *Quinto*. Universal Music Portugal 00602547422712, 2015.

Venues in Lisbon, Portugal

Fado Museum (Museu do Fado). www.museudofado.pt/en.

Casa-Museu Amália Rodrigues. amaliarodrigues.pt/casa-museu/.

Café Luso. www.cafeluso.pt/en/.

Mesa das Frades. www.facebook.com/mesadefradeslisboa.

Tasca do Jaime d'Alfama. www.facebook.com/pages/Tasca-Do-Jaime -Dalfama/595710723791760.

Parreirinha de Alfama. www.parreirinhadealfama.com/en/.

Acknowledgments

THANKS TO: Charles Simard, Kevin Williams, Spencer Williams, and the staff at Talonbooks, Mercedes Bátiz-Benét and Judd Palmer at Puente Theatre, Donna Spencer and Susan Pearl Shank and the staff at the Firehall Arts Centre, Heidi Taylor, Kathleen Flaherty, Belinda Bruce, and Melanie Yeats at the Playwrights Theatre Centre, Kathleen Weiss, Oona Patrick and the Disquiet International Literary Program in Lisbon, Katherine Vaz, Christopher Cerf, Jeff Parker, Scott Laughlin, Jacqueline Goldfinger, Brendan Bowles, Ryan Oliveira, Maggie Felisberto, Alexandrina André, Lídia Saragaço, the British Columbia Arts Council, the Canada Council for the Arts, the Portuguese Cultural Centre of BC, Catherine Banks, Richard Henriquez, Manuel Azevedo, the Consulado Geral de Portugal em Vancouver and Consul Dra. Marta Cowling, Charlie Haden, Suzan-Lori Parks, 50 Playwrights Project, Dr. Trevor Boffone, Dr. Brian Eugenio Herrera, the Playwrights Guild of Canada's Women's Caucus, the Greater Victoria Regional Arts Awards, Filipe Valle Costa and Diogo Martins of Saudade Theatre in New York, Bill Clark, Juno Avila-Clark, Jeff Warren and Quest University Canada, Nuno Cristo, Aida Jordão, Angela Ferreira Cowart, the Caravan Farm Theatre, Carmen Aguirre, Hiro Kanagawa, Dave Deveau, Adrienne Wong, Quelemia Sparrow, Tom Pickett, Lucia Frangione, Mary Anne Santos Newhall, Paulo Ribeiro, Davey Samuel Calderon and Ron Samworth, Luisa Jojic, Lisa Goebel, Maria João Cruz, Paul Moniz de Sá, Ana Ribeiro, Valeria Avina, Gonçalo Ruivo, Margarida André, Alex Hernandez, Jacqueline Guillén, Dylan Kammerer, Cris Oliveira, Benjamin Manno, Nicole Amaral, Alexandra Lainfiesta and Michael Scholar Jr., Stephanie Berkmann, Roy Surette, Matthew Payne, Beira Mar Importers Co. Ltd., Habitat Insurance Agencies, Jovanni Sy, Leanna Brodie, Shawn Macdonald, Meghan Gardiner, Fei Shi, Lila Ellen Gray, Rui Vieira Nery, Fulbright Portugal, Gloria Botelho, Cynthia Reis, Terry Costa at the Encontro Pedras Negras Festival, Nina Soulimant of Associação Reinventar Ilhas, the U.S. Consul General of Ponta Delgada and Principal Officer Kathryn Hammond, Carolina Cordeiro, Susana C. Júdice, Pedro Paulo Câmara, Pieter and Rini Adriaans, Diniz Borges of the Portuguese Beyond Borders Institute, Rod Clarke and Kim Koch of the Paper Hound Bookshop, Jose and Lina Ávila, and my grandparents João Henrique Ávila and Arlina Garcia da Terra Ávila.

Elaine Ávila's plays are produced in Central and Latin America, Europe, the United States, Canada, and Australia. She has received Best New Play Awards for *Jane Austen, Action Figure* (Festival de Los Cocos, Panamá City), *Lieutenant Nun* (Victoria Critics Circle), and *Café a Brasileira* (Disquiet International Literary Program in Lisbon). Her creative non-fiction is published by York University Press, Routledge, Theatre Communications Group, NoPassport Press, Smith and Kraus, *enRoute, HowlRound, Canadian Theatre Review, American Theater, Portuguese American Review, Lusitania, Contemporary Theatre Review,* and *Café Onda.* Teaching in universities from Portugal to lutruwita (Tasmania), China to Panamá, Elaine has served as the playwright-in-residence at Pomona College in Los Angeles, Quest University Canada, and Western Washington University; as the Endowed Chair and Head of the MFA Program in Dramatic Writing at the University of New Mexico; and as founder of the LEAP Playwriting Program at the Arts Club Theatre in Vancouver. With Chantal Bilodeau and Caridad Svich, she is the co-founder of the International Climate Change Theatre Action, involving fifty playwrights, two hundred venues, and twelve thousand audience members worldwide. The 2019 Fulbright Scholar to the University of the Azores, Elaine lives in New Westminster, British Columbia, with her musician-teacher husband and her seventeen-year-old, a core leader of Sustainabiliteens.